ABOUT MAGIC READERS

ABDO continues its commitment to quality books with the nonfiction Magic Readers series. This series includes three levels of books to help students progress to being independent readers while learning factual information. Different levels are intended to reflect the stages of reading in the early grades, helping to select the best level for each individual student.

Level 1: Books with short sentences and familiar words or patterns to share with children who are beginning to understand how letters and sounds go together.

Level 2: Books with longer words and sentences and more complex language patterns with less repetition for progressing readers who are practicing common words and letter sounds.

Level 3: Books with more developed language and vocabulary for transitional readers who are using strategies to figure out unknown words and are ready to learn information more independently.

These nonfiction readers are aligned with the Common Core State Standards progression of literacy, following the sequence of skills and increasing the difficulty of language while engaging the curious minds of young children. These books also reflect the increasing importance of reading informational material in the early grades. They encourage children to read for fun and to learn!

Hannah E. Tolles, MA Reading Specialist

www.abdopublishing.com

Published by Magic Wagon, a division of ABDO, PO Box 398166, Minneapolis, Minnesota 55439. Copyright © 2015 by Abdo Consulting Group, Inc. International copyrights reserved in all countries. No part of this book may be reproduced in any form without written permission from the publisher. Magic Readers™ is a trademark and logo of Magic Wagon.

Printed in the United States of America, North Mankato, Minnesota.
042014
092014

THIS BOOK CONTAINS RECYCLED MATERIALS

Cover Photo: Thinkstock
Interior Photos: Getty Images, Science Source, Shutterstock, Thinkstock

Written and edited by Rochelle Baltzer, Heidi M. D. Elston,
    Megan M. Gunderson, and Bridget O'Brien
Illustrated by Candice Keimig
Designed by Candice Keimig and Jillian O'Brien

Library of Congress Cataloging-in-Publication Data

Elston, Heidi M. D., 1979- author.
  Buffaloes on the prairie / written and edited by Heidi M.D. Elston [and three others] ; designed and illustrated by Candice Keimig.
    pages cm. -- (Magic readers. Level 3)
  Audience: Ages 5-8.
  ISBN 978-1-62402-062-9
1. American bison--Juvenile literature. I. Keimig, Candice, illustrator. II. Title.
QL737.U53E475 2015
  599.64'3--dc23
                    2014005838

Buffaloes
on the Prairie

By Heidi M. D. Elston
Illustrated photos by Candice Keimig

Magic Readers

An Imprint of Magic Wagon
www.abdopublishing.com

Buffaloes live in North America.

They live on the prairie. They also
live in river valleys and forests.

Buffaloes are the largest land animals in North America.

They share the land with prairie dogs, snakes, and birds.

Buffaloes have strong senses of smell and hearing.

This helps them watch out for predators on the prairie.

Wolves, coyotes, mountain lions, and grizzly bears hunt buffaloes.

Wolves

Coyotes

Mountain Lions

Grizzly Bears

Buffaloes are safer in herds than they are alone.

Buffaloes stampede!

In winter, the buffalo's heavy coat helps keep it warm.

Sometimes, there is deep snow.
Then, the buffalo uses its head as
a snowplow.

In spring, the buffalo sheds its
heavy coat.

It rubs against trees or posts. It is left with a lighter spring coat.

In warm weather, buffaloes wallow. They roll back and forth in the dirt.

This gets dirt into their coat. It protects them from bugs and the heat.

As seasons change, buffaloes
move to look for food.

They move from place to place.
This is called migrating.

Many buffaloes live in national parks.

They sometimes travel on roads. So, cars must wait for them to pass.

People love to see buffaloes in the wild!